Swallowing t^h T

SWALLOWING
THE ENTIRE OCEAN

Henry Normal

Flapjack Press
www.flapjackpress.co.uk

Exploring the synergy between performance and the page

Published in 2019 by Flapjack Press
Salford, Gtr Manchester
www.flapjackpress.co.uk

ISBN 978-1-9996707-8-8

Cover art by Johnny Carroll-Pell
Facebook: Art By Johnny
Photographs courtesy of the author

Printed by Imprint Digital
Upton Pyne, Exeter, Devon
imprintdigital.com

**City of
Literature**

Dedicated to Pete Ramskill
for his friendship, inspiration and big big laughs.

I would like to thank Linda Hallam, Paul Neads, Theresa Sowerby, Penny Shepherd and my wife Angela Pell for their help in bringing this collection together.

Contents

"I seem to have been only like a boy playing on the sea-shore, and diverting myself in now and then finding a smoother pebble or a prettier shell than ordinary, whilst the great ocean of truth lay all undiscovered before me."

Sir Isaac Newton FRS PRS

Swallowing the Entire Ocean

I am Henry

Not the Henry that sucks up dust
Not Henry the serial queen murderer
Not Henry the splash it all over
    almost beat Muhammad Ali with one punch
Not Henry the Fourth Part One
    or Part Two
Not little Prince Harry grown up now reverting to his real name
Not Thomas the Tank Engine's work colleague
Not Henry the Navigator, Henry the droopy faced dog,
Not Adrian Henry, Lenny Henry or Thierry Henri
mispronounced

I am

Henry the filler of dishwashers
Henry the reluctant shopper
Henry the surveyor of parameters
Henry the functional
Henry the spotter of patterns
Henry the dad, the husband,
    the brother, the son, the friend
Henry the retired
Henry that sucks up dust now I come to think of it
Henry the yet to be fully defined

Some people

Some people will be wondering if everything
in the show tonight will be in rhyme
and have now worked out that it won't

Some people will be wondering if everything
in the show tonight will be funny
and have now worked out that it won't

Some people will be wondering if everything
in the show tonight will be repetitive
No – it won't

Some people will be wondering
if it will be too cerebral

Some people will be wondering
what the word cerebral means

Some people have already decided
that this is not proper poetry

Some people are now feeling pretty smug
about their own poetry

Some people will be wondering
whether there's anyone in the audience
they can fantasise about having sex with
whilst pretending to listen to this 'so called' poetry

Some people will be wondering
if they should have gone to the toilet before

Some people will be wondering
if they should have gone to the toilet instead

Some people are here because
they only came with a partner or friend
and are now re-evaluating that relationship
and their opinions

Some people are here because
they don't have a partner or friend or relationships
or opinions

Some people will be wondering
if they should be insulted by that last joke

Some people are now a little uncomfortable that
I've mentioned the word joke in a poem
which is confusing

Some people will be wondering
why I didn't stop this poem 10 lines ago
when it peaked

Some people will be wondering
if I even know what they're wondering
and wonder whether they even know
what they are wondering half the time

Some people will be wondering
if I'm just wondering about myself
and my own wonderings
about other people
and don't realise those other people
have stopped laughing
and are just wondering

Some people will be wondering
if this is his only poem
or if it's his best poem
or emblematic of his poetry as a whole
or if it is not in fact a poem at all
as they originally suspected

Some people will be wondering
why he's suddenly started referring to himself
in the third person

and when it's done
some people will be wondering

should we clap?

Complication

White and pink blossom
on the same tree

its effect
like raspberry ripple

or if you count the trunk
Neapolitan gateau

I have to look closely
to be sure

trace each laden twig
back to the root

I've seen this phenomenon once before
on my small sapling at home

Mostly covered with white
flowers

on one low branch pink petals
had begun to bloom until

I snapped it off

Perhaps to simplify the aesthetic
or to unclutter my thoughts
or just to fit in

Or maybe embarrassed
that its difference would say
something
about my complication

I can hear my son enjoying colour

Rainbows hide
in white light

Burnt chicory hangs sweet in the air
There's not a blemish in this February sky

I scrunch up my shorts
to capture more sunshine on my thighs

There's no pressure to enjoy myself
so at last I can relax and enjoy myself

The thermometer never gets a minute's rest
Each breeze tests its metal

We have a tree that's not decided yet
whether it's lime or lemon

I expose my lower back to the sun
and try to gauge the optimum duration

to balance risk and benefit
My scars look better with a tan

A nearby bird machine-sews a hem
with a hundred sides

Angela sings as she slices tomatoes and onion
Japanese tea warms my throat

I am not without pain
but it is proportionate

with the age of my joints
and the decay of my sinews

I'm conscious that my bladder
seems on permanent amber

Though
today will not go down in any history books

if we were to chart happiness
this is a day to remember

Nature versus synthetic polymers

There are three things made of plastic in my garden –
a football sitting by the swing

my mobile
and the biro nuzzling my knuckles

Four – as I notice the soles on my Doc Martens
My body comes in useful as a sun shield for my iPhone

Ants are already exploring the edges of things
Brown paper leaves curl on a plant defiantly off-season

Five – I forgot the frames of my glasses
When the breeze drops the heat bakes flesh undisguised

An aphid accelerates past my ear on a very small Vespa
Trees stand ready with knuckles like pugilists

The lemon daffodils
are so perfect they could be man-made

In another world gardeners and farmers
would be priests

The Mona Lisa probably wouldn't have had the same impact if Leonardo had painted the back of her head

The strange thing about a selfie
is you are often not looking at the camera

You are looking at the phone
but the camera is in the corner

You are looking at the bit of the phone where
you are going to be looking at the photo

As though the screen was taking the picture
rather than the lens

Like looking at a canvas
rather than the portrait artist

The effect is that it feels as though the viewer
is to the side watching someone take a selfie

There is no eye
contact

like someone peering over your shoulder
or avoiding their own gaze in the mirror

A boy can clap louder than the breakers

There is no better place
and no worse place to be ill
than on holiday

I have bent my book out of shape

The warmth on my chest
penetrates the tissues

Looking out across damp crags
to the headlands beyond
smoothed with scorched grass
time becomes irrelevant

A million creatures had to live to give me this life

If I sit at the very corner
I can enjoy two beaches
with perfect vantage
like a lifeguard

Two towels underneath me
take the edge off jagged lava

Those I love are out there somewhere
It is only a matter of steps

The sea takes a run up
to try and intimidate the cliff face
in an age-old argument

It's sad to think
this page has become a barrier
between us

Angela tells me to generalise such images
to relate to more people
but I am anchored to the particular

Sometimes when she frowns
without knowing
two vertical lines
appear between her eyebrows

Though we spin at the same speed
we don't put our arms around each other
as much as I'd like

and when she takes my hand for no reason
I'm not always ready to share

A girl with a limp shuffles across the beach
leaving a distinctive trail

An aircraft carrier has parked overhead
A flotilla of tugs surround it

The sand starts to darken
one drop at a time

Our other life is
as far away as tomorrow's weather

Dry humour – a cautionary verse

Wet suits are hard to put on
tightness is part of their charm
but too tight is the one you try to don
by putting your leg through the arm

Brighton nudist beach twinned with Vila do Bispo nudist beach

Aside from the sand
and the all-over tans
There's very little difference at all
It is less cold so
in Vila do Bispo
the scrotums are not so small

Terminal

There's free alcohol samples for breakfast
An ice cream bigger than a child's face

Heads propped up by elbows
Jumpers tied around waists

Last minute tat on tap
Exclusive membership of the club sandwich

I try to hold onto my humanity
and a small hope of tenderness amid

the easy welcome of
wipe-clean formica

Utility
as Utopia

barely masking a production line
worthy of Temple Grandin

It is impossible to get home
without passing a Toblerone

We are the souls left in ASDA
after the rapture

You can inhale the dead man's fingers from the car park

My son applauds the sea
the sky and the whole shebang

He takes his time before
dipping his shoulders

His mum models
bravery and commitment

They float with feet touching
like Neptune's bookends

This high pressure is in its twelfth week
Boats have left the marina for the first time in years

I sit with Johnny's abandoned tee shirt over my head
Henry of Arabia

The Sussex stones become ball bearings
underfoot

We pop the seaweed like bubble wrap
and lick ice lollies from our wrists

A near-naked old lady cake-walks the slope
as though alcohol just reached her legs

Her dog squats in front of us and shits upwind
then wanders into the water to wash his backside

The old lady and her near-naked mum make camp

They put up a large umbrella
like a tall man
sitting on the seat directly in front at the cinema
wearing a top hat

The universe is telling us something

Once in the car a thunderstorm
pisses its full bladder

An entire ocean falling from Heaven

causing everyone to try to remember
which windows they've left open

Through my car windscreen in the rain
I can recreate impressionism

Lines approximate themselves
bending round and over droplets

Shapes fudge their edges
in a universal squint

A trio of water butts
become three dabs
from a small palette knife

Planks become waves
Doors – bite marks

If I move my head to and fro
a surf rolls along the fence

The side of the shed bulges like an alien
moving under skin

Not unlike the Grand Old Duke of York
but without the ten thousand men

Beyond the reach of satellites
I'm standing alone
trying to communicate

Halfway up a hill
I'm hoping
the signal bends enough to compensate

Over
hedgerows impersonating a mess of wires
I notice moss on the roofs of farm houses

Fields curve away in all directions
Tractor tracks resemble waffles
I cross the cattle grid and I have bars

Through the leaves of a distant sycamore
I can see the blades of a windmill
waving

Where tarmac has become dirt
amongst nettles and ivy
I hold plastic and metal to my ear

Even
at the sound of the phone in the hall ringing
                              I am home

Thundersnow sails in from France
leaving footprints on my kitchen floor

There's a penguin on the lawn
unable to huddle

It takes a lot of frozen hexagons to make a snowman
just half the shovelling for a snowbird

A nose becomes a beak
my dark gloves form wings

It's so cold out
even dogs and horses wear coats

Icicles hang like evil teeth
Only hot chocolate can save us

Antifreeze
should have entered the engine yesterday

I pass cooling towers with grey hair
rising against the descent

The train smells of damp students
A snowdrift has us reversing

My toes are snow-blind
My eyes have frostbite

My phone has drained its battery
I am on my own

This passing landscape is bleached coral
A blackbird defies the dress code

We are meltwater
searching for an estuary

I realise now I missed my peak
worrying about feeling inadequate

I see a blind man
with a stick the colour of snow

Permanent marker doesn't work on wet sand

If I were sitting on this beach alone
I would be self-conscious

but my family are displacing
sea water to waist level

so I think nothing of scribbling
amongst clothes strewn across boulders

I am not apart
I am in relation

I am not defined by onlookers but by
knowledge of function and motivation

I am part of something bigger
I am part of a shared experience

between the elements
and those I love

Poseidon threatens
falling at our feet

like an aggressive drunk
who doesn't really want a fight

Twenty yards in front
water arcs above our heads

our clothes strategically placed behind us
in case the tide lurches

We can taste the salt on our lips

each wave thwarted
by the previous one retreating

This rage is not at us
it is for us

Paranoia

Seagulls love to shit
down my window

It takes some effort
There's nowhere to perch

so they must have to
veer in flight

and without colliding
into glass or surround

with skater-like grace
curve and curl up and away

risking damage or mortality
in order to precision bomb

Given the number of places
to excrete in the world

and the amount of off-white
on my window

there's either one
dedicated defecator

or an elaborate avian
conspiracy

Maybe guano
is evenly distributed around the globe

and I am just more conscious
when it obscures my view

The idea that a creature would migrate
thousands of miles crossing continents

specifically to irritate me
is impressive

Maybe it's gull guerrilla
street art

or maybe the birds are simply scared
by their own reflection

The thinnest of rain

Like invisible fish
kissing the air

I can only see the consequence
on the surface of the pool at first

then minute acupuncture targets
my sun-creamed back

pins too fine and too fast
for any amateur eye

ghost as a lover's whimper
until all is quiet

Suspects saunter above
as innocent as Heaven

Sea level and water vapour on high
again lead their separate lives

I take the twenty-first century into my garden

It's already there of course

From a child's swing I see
the tall grass offers affirmation

though there's not breeze enough
to challenge the rust on the windmill

I'm unsure whether it's orange blossom
or honeysuckle that sweetens the air

Certain seagulls seem too large to fly
as if pillows with wings

The fuselage of a jet catching the sun
becomes a torpedo or missile

Chives and ornamental thistles show
nature is not ashamed to stand phallic

The hose lurks on the lawn
a snake playing dead

The olive trees have formed a hedge
Bamboo now encircles the trampoline

A lone butterfly white as a moth
tacks its way through lavender

The silver birch at the focal point
leans

like it's giving summer a high five

Line from a commuted sentence

Sidings cut back in December still smart
Tunnels show those on work calls who's boss

Council houses sport conservatories
with extensive views of the track

Pylons stand like Samurai warriors
We are too sedate for a Turner painting

A southbound train passes too close
to focus on any single window

like trying to spot an individual card
during a shuffle

A concrete field of cars suggests Gatwick
Industrial litter confirms it

We pull out past trees
favouring their amputations

and an assortment of fences representing
discontinued styles from recent decades

Above our heads the digital display keeps alive
the forgotten dreams of Teletext

Yellow diggers wait
for matching hats

Puddles appear in shapes
like a Rorschach test

A motorway disappears underneath
as quick as a rat in a kitchen

A different line arches away
to unknown adventures

There's more stone chippings here
than any garden centre could cope with

A single flag of St. George curls in on itself
Solar panels patch south-facing roofs

Trees auditioning for nightmares
wait for the dark

In their upper branches
birds' nests lie like dead pom-poms

Freight trains manage to look
both futuristic and mundane

Anarchic architecture announces East Croyden
like a blind man's sock drawer

Graffiti-tags succeed in taking the bland
and making it worse

Mobile phone masts reach for the sky
as thin metal cathedrals

There's one lone man sitting on a bench
looking out at an empty field

then solid brickwork forming a film set
from the inside of a headache

This is Clapham Junction
a robot guard admits

Rain hits platform 13
unlucky for some

Over unused chimneys
Lego tower blocks lurk like tombstones

See it, say it, sort it
The tannoy announces

We enter London Victoria
as though commencing a colonoscopy

It looks like God bought more green paint than he needed

It's not all the same green

Even with the grass
the tone varies

Clumps are khaki
New shoots edge towards lime

When discerning a particular hue
the size and shape of leaves can

deceive the eye
as does light itself

The undergrowth and inner branches
are naturally darker

There's a songbird somewhere in the shade
insisting it has something to say

Footprints and hoofprints
lie together in bare mud

sometimes parallel
sometimes overlaid

Dandelions spot the field
like floral acne

No-one has told the insects
this is wasteground

Steam spaceships push
against the spin of the earth with
little hope of out-running the night

Plotting to invade as rain
they glory in their air superiority
like an ocean on the move

They lord the sky smiling down
on the vanity of water-based humans
already searching for cover

Poem in the shape of an arts grant application

1a. To whomsoever sits in judgement
on the dishing out of other people's money
based on the completion of preset forms

2a. I'd like to apply for a grant
to complete next year's grant application papers
over a period of twelve months
exclusive of any further endeavour

3a. I guarantee to produce no work of benefit
to the public other than the perpetual
funding of my own application process

4a. I promise to fully monitor and record this process
and file the essential completed feedback forms throughout

4b. The documentation of my documentation
will involve the highest creative excellence
without the worry of adverse consumer reaction
or public perception
being completely inwardly focussed

5a. I would confirm I am an equal opportunity grantee
and promise to take money off any Arts Organisation
irrespective of class, creed, colour, nationality,
physical or mental ability, gender or sexual orientation

6a. It is my hope that your commitment to this ambitious project
(albeit merely financially)
will serve to help demystify the funding process
and thereby demystify the arts themselves
at the very least
to me

6b. I realise this is not an original idea
6b. (supplementary) so I believe it should present no difficulties

The inflatable shop

The shop itself is not inflatable
It sells inflatables

An eight foot lobster
is the first to catch your eye

strapped upright to a terracotta pillar
its pincers reaching for Heaven

it shivers in the Algarve breeze
The air inside is contained

There are black handles on its back
to help you ride it in the water

A giant yellow rubber duck
sits alongside

as if for an oversized bath
or indeed, a pool

Nearby
the pink flamingo is without long legs

made to be only the bit you see sitting
above the water

That is, if you were ever to see
a flamingo sitting on some water

Then there's a rubber ring made to look like
a doughnut

behind which there's a dinghy, a seahorse
and a waterbed with a plastic cup holder

Finally, I notice a blow-up plastic shape I'd never seen before
A six foot wide pizza slice

sporting pictures of tomatoes, mushrooms, olives,
red peppers and onion rings

I am waiting across the car park
next to the dead stump of a former tree

which is now completely covered
with wild flowers

A wealth of tiny purple petals and a few
straggly white weeds make it perfectly untidy

On a break, the shop owner stands outside
cradling a cigarette

He draws breath
smoke inflating his lungs

The saddest line I've ever written

The girl that I thought my true love
who I had lived with for 3 years
on my birthday
handed me
an unwrapped
box of Roses chocolates

As bleak as February
before my next birthday
across the peaks and home
my eyes flooded the road
as I returned the removal van
empty

(of course
I
would
have
preferred
Quality Street)

Apologies

The poet sends his sincere apologies
that he will not be able to be present
for tonight's performance

Well not in the way he'd like

The funny poet you remember
or maybe you don't
fears he can't live up to expectations

The serious poet he feels he should be
never existed
and most likely never will

The happy poet
on the best day of his life
surrounded by love and family

a sense of fulfilment and well-being
was too present
to put pen to paper

The actual poet that wrote these lines
is a little embarrassed to appear himself
so he sent me to stand in his stead

the responsible poet
the guarded yet vulnerable human poet
the work-in-progress

Lightly poached

One huge grey cloud now hangs over holidaymakers
like a sunshade

Sneers on the well oiled
pay no heed to the heatwave warnings

some no longer easy over
some no longer sunny side up

the parade of shapes surprised
by the north wind

We risk the collapse of sandstone
at the far end of the stretch

to find our own space
late in the afternoon

Humanity at a distance
appears more poetic

A few spots of rain matter little
once you're immersed in seawater

There's another autistic kid in the waves
who's also wearing ear defenders

We notice the similarities
and the differences

Johnny plays avalanches
on the sharp edge of the sand bank

Angela
brings sweet orange juice from the café

The tall shadow moves towards
America

The cliff
fails to collapse

Save me from myself

This is a lot to ask
Too much
as I hardly know you

So I ask if you
will sleep with me

hiding behind
an obvious failing

To be rejected for
only a partial
inadequacy

is easier to bear

Abusive body language

You sit with your arms crossed
defensive like a portcullis

You could be hugging yourself
for comfort

Your hand supports your chin
the first two fingers giving me the V sign

It could be a comfortable position for you or
an intention to display curiosity or interest

Your index finger sits before your mouth
as though stopping yourself from speaking

You hang at the door
half in half out seemingly
judging each sentence
to see whether it is worth staying

teetering on each individual word

Your middle finger pushes back your glasses
pointedly giving me the bird
and I wonder if you'd display that gesture
without specs

I take off my own glasses and demonstrate

It is only when you laugh
I know I can relax

though I listen carefully
to ensure the sound is not hollow

By decree

At fifteen minutes past the hour
there will be no 'other'

Everything will be 'one'

This is not to say that anything
will physically change

but all will be required by law
to perceive the change

Those who wish to perceive the change earlier
may do so

Those missing the deadline
will have up to 4 minutes to comply

The change will be permanent
and will be ruthlessly enforced
upon the one entity
by itself

It is an all or nothing scenario
There is only one choice

There will be no other

Fixing a problem that doesn't exist

An empty car rolls backwards in the car park
threatening collision

Three passers-by halt its progress
and push the escapee back into its spot

The driver returns and concedes
this is not the first time wanderlust has occurred

"This model
is going back to the old style handbrake"
he explains

"They've fixed a problem
that didn't exist"
he jokes

Later
when he leaves
the driver gives me the thumbs up

mistaking me for one of the helpers

I return the gesture

there's no use in trying to explain

Foreword for a book of poetry I have not actually read

We have here a collection of poems
the likes of which
I've never seen

The first poem starts us off
and from then on it's non-stop poems
as poem after poem comes at you
one after another, verse after verse,
until there is simply no more to be read

In essence
it is a grouping of symbols we call 'letters'
fashioned with some element of skill into 'words'
styled into an arrangement called lines
These lines then build into structual
entities considered 'poems'
by the author
and are then placed on pages
in numerically ascending order
to form what is regarded
or more often than not disregarded
as a 'poetry book'

With a contents page
at the front and
copyright naming this author
I can categorically state
this particular collection forms
a book
unlike any other
by this publisher

in this font
with its
unique ISBN number

Books like this need to be read
to be appreciated and understood

What I can say is that barring loss or damage
this is a collection you can
read again and again
technically

I must admit to this day
merely the sight of the cover alone
leaves me asking questions

I am more than certain
there's nothing I can honestly tell you
that can capture the experience
of actually
reading these poems
for yourself

This thing that was once me is now the property of others

Of course
I never actually owned anything
I've merely been borrowing these atoms

Only this consciousness is mine
and when it no longer has a home
I can be said to have ended

A single tear in the ribbon lake
A small ripple in all directions
lost in the deluge

If you look carefully though
for the briefest of moments
there is an effect
on all that is close

and possibly even

a wave
breaking
somewhere
on a
distant
embankment

The house is so clean and tidy
if I were to die now
it would be convenient for all concerned
apart from me, of course

I have an hour
before my next responsibility
and if I can avert death for this period
I have myself an unexpected bonus

Yes, there are things
to be done in the future
but not
for the next sixty minutes

I can sit and watch the waves
busy clambering nowhere
A bird outside my window
sounds like a new born lamb

If I lay my head down
the horizon becomes vertical
Land and sea just east and west
and I wonder which eye will close first

The Marathon as viewed by an ex-sprinter

Breathless I stand
with humanity
lapping me

Amid the runners
I can't help but pick out
those older than myself

Even on my best day
with the best equipment
I'd struggle

Those in fancy dress
just seem to be
taking the piss

Each morning
I now have to sit
to put on my socks

Between these lines
there is nothing
that appeals

Neither oxygen
nor water
has a taste

making it easier
to spot what shouldn't
be there

Lost in the numbers
I envy most
the sense of connection

I get tired these days
watching the sun move across the sky

Queen Victoria and her Nottingham lace stockings

Albert removed the royal lace
whilst Victoria she would sit
From the number of kids they had
he did that quite a bit

Privates' progress

En suite
replacing outside loo
From the luxury of your own silk sheets
you can hear your partner poo

Landfill

I am many years older than my mother
but this morning I am older than my brother
and I wake in pain

Mountain Pass
is somewhat an ironic name
for a road this narrow

The Atlantic
does its impression
of liquid time

A man without a skin complaint
drops his girlfriend playfully
into the big wet

I'm old enough to know that all the oceans
are really just one body of water
that has no name itself

People all around are enjoying
their physical forms
giving their tattoos air

Water dances around solids

A man my age and half again
wishes me a happy birthday

You might think this the still
of early evening

but assorted birds compete in song
like an overdue dawn chorus

Overhead a cornflower canvas
is brushed with watercolours

as it nears the horizon
becoming smudges of pink and white

Gulls lope from one roof to another
seemingly without reason

On the top of the trellis
a lone magpie spars with the invisible

ducking his head
as if dodging a blow

Insects too small and too quick to identify
play with my peripheral vision

A Jumbo Jet close to Heaven boasts
its bass tones

I can hear the coast road
sighing with late traffic

Different sizes and shapes of silhouette
making little or no sound

wing their way
from one point of the compass to another

The sea though low
never allows itself rest

Night calls
from ever more distant gardens

If I sit with one leg crossed over my knee
it rises and falls with my pulse

Should my l ttle scratches surv ve my bones
outlast ng flood and explos on
eros on and other vandals

then
g ve
pause

n a colder cl mate, learn ng
n danger and n fear
 am more than absent flesh

A compendium of woes

Not antique
we are vintage

Pre-loved

From plum to prune
our world has shrunk inside our clothes

Where once sleep healed
new pains greet the day

Time
has become a faulty immune system

We are over-conscious of anatomy
in a conspiracy of internal landscape

Even where appearance presents the same
strength is missing

We are flimsy like painted scenery
or a chocolate egg

Tiredness leaves us intolerant to movement
and slows ambition

Activity that was once so vital
now belongs to others

Enjoy the lairiness of youth
and the smugness of middle age

If you live long enough
you will join us

one ailment at a time

There was naturally
apprehension at the start
but the audience soon settled
and became worthy of this great poet

Henry's charismatic presence and assured presentation
coupled with his unequalled modesty
helped those unfamiliar with the subtle sophistication
of his poetry to relax and in some cases orgasm

Towards the latter stages
a few deluded fools
were still not convinced
by the awesome power
of Henry's lyrical invention
but even these diehard traditionalists
at the end, humbled and apologetic
had to admit
often through uncontrollable tears
and self-flagellation
that their whole concept
of what was possible in poetry
had been changed

and that they
pitiful and pathetic
as they were
cowed and shamefaced
had now been forced to reasses
not only their misguided view of creativity
but their entire hitherto wasted existence

In repentance some former critics
savagely ripped out their own tongues
and hacked off their typing fingers
leaving their writing hands
as bleeding festering stumps
which Henry insisted was unnecessary
though wholly understandable
(if a bit attention seeking)

There were calls for Henry to be
given an OBE, a Knighthood, The Freedom of Newhaven,
a Dukedom, an Earldom, a Duke of Earl-dom,
World Laureate, Emperor, Pontiff, Messiah, Greatest Human Ever,
Best Mammal and Best Known Life Form (in any category)

Poetry Please received so many requests for his work
it is to be renamed *Henry Please*

Unable to hold back
aliens finally decided
this was the right moment to make themselves visible
in order to give this 'People's Poet' the standing ovation
throughout the universe that he deserves

The sun and the moon were seen to wink at each other knowingly

The Milky Way did a high five with Andromeda

and all the gods that had ever been invented
bowed their heads in recognition

Even the Big Bang had to concede
it had been outdone

Five trillion stars, a smiley face and a thumbs up
PN Review

The romance of the Brontës

Talking in a car outside Howarth
you toy with the notion of getting married

I know you are still in love with your ex
so there is no ring of truth to this proposal

Later in that same vehicle
I hear a love song on the radio

and realise it's not you
I'm singing to

The fug of abstraction

Cloud lounges on the ground
but only in the valleys

Not a teaspoon of rain this July

Steam from a kettle
is par for the course

as golfers hotfoot
to the 18th yellow

New perennials
might not live up to the name

Trigger happy I shoot
the lone Hydrangeas

A collared dove complains
from the cheap seats

Wallflowers
await the firing squad

whilst my in-laws' market garden
doses in its raised beds

I say potato
you say Solanum Tuberosum

I say tomato
you say Solanum Lycopersicum

One thing I know for certain
lettuces would be easier to water
if it wasn't for the leaves

Half baked

Though my intention
is to paddle to my knees
the elements have other plans

Wind goads the water
way out in the gulf stream

We tiptoe the swell in unison
and this is the closest I get
to dancing

The ground shifts
under my feet
as the sea gives and takes

Shape, size and shade
all remind me
of the need for balance

A mother takes too many photos
of her mermaid daughter
beached

The daughter
takes none
of her mother

A bather stares back
to see if his stuff is safe
under the umbrella

Synchronised sun worship
doesn't sit easy with me
I fear losing myself in the in-crowd

Whatever it is I lack
I hope it is individual

Older souls explore the rock falls
at the lonely end
of this open bay

Young couples
dive head first
through the oncoming

or turn their backs
to the shove

Vision at Porches, Lagoa

Frogs and goldfish avoid eye contact
Birdsong leaks from hidden branches
Bees collide into climbers unconcerned

Small peaches tempt, already pelt-like to the touch
Orange blossom intoxicates
There's an almost tangible taste of wood burning in a grate

We divert with humous, pitta and family photos
under sun-speckled arches classically carved
My son skips, captivated by handcrafted heritage

The daughters of fishermen and farmers
tame the pale blue of an April sky
the muted green of an olive tree

A hint of Heaven
by human design

The most interesting thing about me

The most interesting thing about me
is not this poem

or any of my poems
not the people I've met

not the things I've achieved
not the loss I've suffered

not the challenges I've overcome
not the love I've experienced

not the details or the emotion
not the consequence

The most interesting thing about me
is that when you said

my name
was the most interesting thing about me

I didn't feel the need to defend my life
my personality or my right to exist

to you who knows nothing of my journey
That is the most interesting thing

at least to me

Theatre in the round

There's a dog squealing
like a squeezy toy
somewhere in suburbia

I wonder if I should have sprinkler envy
as I watch next door's garden being hydrated
with almost military precision

My fluid anarchy
has its plus points
I convince myself

I still dream of an air strike
taking out the tall chimneys
between me and a perfect horizon

Behind wide leaf curtains
mopeds fart along
to the nearby junction

Young kittiwakes
argue constantly
over nothing

One sits on the spikes
around a neighbour's gutter balancing
out of sheer bloody mindedness

Sunshine has abandoned the grass
and now flirts with roof tiles
and the westward tips of trees

A procession of starlings
on their way to greater glory
form a mobile dot to dot

A cloud
in the shape of a fishbone
dangles in the blue

Crows alarm
like something mechanical
is in error

A unicorn takes to the sea

A mother and her daughter struggle
to mount the mythical creature

as waves buck
wild and unbroken

A sullen boy still in baseball cap and trainers
refuses to enjoy the heatwave

A teenage girl models her bright orange dress
against the blue

A lone bald man leaves his collapsible chair
and makes friends with the ocean

We are with young families and the aged
a colour chart of pink and brown

The big man sporting his small fishing rod
wanders away with his pockmarked wife

If I had an extra fifteen seconds of life
I'm sure I wouldn't want to spend it arguing
who was first in the queue

A rented cremation

The vicar at my brother's funeral
was a bit full of himself

seemingly on a strict time schedule
with us just another set of mourners

Punters
as you might say if this were show business

It took me a while to settle
into these temporary surroundings

sanitised, austere, but
functionally respectful
Candles with ribbons and dried flowers

My brother had been
trying to learn a new piece of guitar music
before he died

I'd downloaded it from iTunes
and here it was
something personal at last

As the melody played I pictured Dave
trying again and again to
master the chords

his fingers bent around the frets

the closing of one eye
on a bum note
as he bit into his plectrum

Then finally
playing
this time perfect

Nothing says siesta like a hammock

This stretch of cloth
finds our new balance
like water readjusting

a gentle sway
a pulse
settling

All I'm missing is a poncho
and a sombrero

The pergola's self-thatching roof
now a horizontal ladder
of timber and wild roses
tops this makeshift cage
for my oversize
budgie's swing

Ivy climbs the trellis
like wall bars
in an abandoned gym

I am a guest
in nature's green room
relaxing at the interval

a pirate
marooned
in paradise

a creature
cocooned
awaiting flight

a jungle soldier
in hiding
long after the war

I am both happy
and sad
about the lack of insects

A bird launches from
a nearby branch
clattering
like a cricket stroke
onto the bails

By far
the hardest part of using a hammock
is getting out

We are a few street lights then only God's mercy

Luz, August 2018

Never have I seen the sea
so black during the day

The ashes of cremated trees
shroud the southern coast

There is no trim to the veil
only blurred vision

Windmills are still turning
moving the dust in circles

On the low hills their red eyes
serve as a warning

Despite the darkness
it is too early for stars

A storm hangs in silence
as the sky can't yet cry

Tourist fodder

I like to savour the minor achievement
of going through an entire day
without buying anything

Still
I'm regretting having not brought my medication
The small of my back itches like it harbours a parasite

I'm unwashed to lock in body heat
and I've got that faraway look
in my React-o-lites

The beggar in the centre of Lagos
is English
I'm not sure why I'm annoyed at him

It is more like June
than St. Valentine's Day
but the sea is not playing along

The main street is closed
awaiting the last leg of a cycle race
We are given free caps advertising loan sharks

Between temporary distractions

I like to concentrate fully on my own mortality
and really get my money's worth
of morbid self-indulgence

My partner
is pleased to be adding paces to her stepometer
as we try to find the ice cream shop

Lumb Bank to St. Thomas à Becket and St. Thomas the Apostle Graveyard, Heptonstall

The steep hill causes me to catch my breath

Old and new words live alongside one another
Bi-fold double-glazed doors overlook farm sheds

Tangled woodland
surrounds saplings in their plastic sheaths

I enter holy ground through Churchyard Bottom
Wood pigeons stand poised on turrets

I'm intrigued by a monkey puzzle tree
and a sign with the vicar's name redacted

The old graveyard is too full of slate
you need to cross the road to new plots

past the fireman at number thirty and the plaque
saying 'Commonwealth War Graves'

A helpful note from the council states
'No rubbish, rubble or waste of any kind'

A magpie teases as though to offer guidance
A bloke from Bradford obliges

He's showing his American friends around
They're "off to Haworth tomorrow"

On one headstone here it said 'Hughes'
but someone has decided that 'Plath' is enough

On one next-door neighbour it says 'Frances Joseph Carr
died 1960 age 61 years'

On the other it says 'Emily Draper
Died 1995 aged 61 years'

There's no age on Sylvia's headstone
just the dates '1932 - 1963'

'Even amid fierce flames
the golden lotus can be planted'

As you step back you notice the new graves
on the front rank freshly dug

and that there's still space for us both

On the way home I meet Duncan
a fellow poet

He'd seen the cemetery before
and is more interested in a cup of tea

He tells me that when he went the first time
he couldn't find Sylvia's gravestone

and wrote a poem about that
which sounds much better than my effort

I'm happy for him
and decide never to write mine

How would you like me to list my ailments?

In alphabetical order?
In chronological order?
In order of annoyance?

In order of severity and possible fatal consequences?
In order of the obscurity of their medical terminology?
In order of likely risk of contagion?

In order of compatibility with your own ailments?
In order of social acceptability?
In order of ease of explanation or ease of spelling?

In order of surface area of skin or volume of body parts affected?
In order of likelihood to induce nausea?
In order of my favourites?

Drought

I'm never sure how I'm supposed to know
if there's a hosepipe ban

As every helicopter or small plane
approaches my air space

my entire being
winces

The heatwave has bleached
the short grass on the slope

It seems no amount of water
will get it to go green

Starting where the first shadows fall
I refresh the roots

I paint the wet
as though spraying an aerosol

firing onto the stubble
like a soggy flame thrower

When it comes to the pots
I worry about over-watering

but every time I test the soil
I touch the surface of the moon

In the absence of an official letter
I choose to be responsible

As the chill moves in I reel back quickly
like a fisherman without a permit

Swelter skelter

Taking my shirt off in public
is not something I'd normally do
even in this heat

On a beach it's fine –
a shopping centre
less so

Perhaps OK here at this secluded farm
or rather in its makeshift car park
waiting for family

I'm conscious of the metal bars
that stretch the fabric on the camping chair
The seat's a size too small in truth

When I move my arm I notice
my skin has indentations
in the shape of Phillips' screw heads

I've taken off my tight trainers
and my striped socks leaving
each exposed hair sensitive to the smallest breeze

This handwriting has become spidery
the sun blotching the black ink
as it falls to the tip of my biro

Looking up I notice
there's a telegraph pole
with no wires

A mite runs the margin
of my notebook
no respecter of literary invention

On closer inspection
the pole has one wire
hidden by nearby branches

It comes from nowhere
and goes at right angles
off to nowhere

A horse's head
hooks over the stable door
like a cartoon of Kilroy

I move my chair
to underneath the foliage
the single line now above my head

From this seated position
the trees beyond the forgotten field
look even taller

The design of their shadows
resembles army camouflage
in monochrome

There's a major city of cloud to the north
Outward-bound holiday-makers
skirt its conurbation in an elegant arc

The echo of the Rolls Royce engine
sounds like the last of the bathwater
being drawn down pipes

It's as though the sky has divided into two halves
The sun keeping goal in one half
whilst cumulonimbus pack the defence in the other

Something local with teeth or a sting
reminds me
I'm a tourist

Unmoved
my Land Rover stands with weeds tickling its
undercarriage

I return the folding chair
to its day job of sliding around
on corners and changes of speed

Losing the ability to float

My feet are in the moat of a sandcastle
as I try to work out if the tide is
coming in or going out

Forest fires now extinguished
we are once again enjoying
the early stages of global warming

People take the trouble
to erect umbrellas on sand
then sit in direct sunlight

Beside a red and yellow flag
a young boy tries
to capture the ocean in a bottle

Face to God
my family backstroke
kicking up a froth

Below the cliff walk
twisted metal being
the remains of the safety fence

resembles the skeleton
of an extinct creature
the sea licking its rusted bones

Exact

In the car park at Sainsbury's
the last of the trolleys huddle together

A retiring sun
glints where rust has not yet taken hold

I adjust to fit my defined oblong
If I could I would restart every conversation

phone again to explain
Reset context and parameters

Like a cold wind on a toothache

I am wearing all my clothes in bed
My coat imitates an eiderdown
still I am chilled to convulsions
up the sides of my spine

I have Tiger Balm in my case
that's looking increasingly enticing
though having to get out of bed to find it
is deterrent enough

Earlier I sat in my car
engine running
with the blower on full
defrosting in the heated seat

The main house is marginally warmer
Perhaps the kitchen is the cosiest
room of all
but others are preparing food

If my fellow guests were to turn
cannibal on me
I would insist on being served
flambé

This thing that helped sailors discover continents

It's strange how so simple a thing
as the movement of air
can make such a show

It competes with the sun
on the surface of skin

teases the top of water
and gives trees a voice

bullies birds and insects
carries seeds, shifts clouds
and orientates animals in fields

fresh-dries clothes and towels
rattles doors and shutters
and messes with my wife's hair

fills lungs with energy
dizzies the brain
and beats ears like a jazz drummer

It's a page turner

Depending on how fast or how forcefully it moves
we give it different names
and wonder how all the palm trees aren't lopsided

It can lift roofs like kites
bend and bow nature
fan the fiercest flames
raise high the high seas
chill God's bones
and punish all in its path

Only the mountains
dare stand their ground

You are no longer alone

You are still there in Spacetime
before the markings on the headstone
before the straightened bedspread
before I lost your voice
before the end

Even in the gaps
between memories
you are there
glorious and alive
and I am with you

A sofa in the dining room

The irony of reading a book
about beautiful trees
doesn't escape me

I feel abused by the faint-hearted
I know I will die working class
fists clenched and one eye on the door

I know you can't fight the ocean
and that greater men than me
have died like kittens

I know I can't do fashionably distressed
and looking back in the early morning snow
I see my father's footprints

I'd sooner sleep in a chair
than lie down in the afternoon
If the line breaks it won't be me

A close relationship unsung

after Wayne Holloway Smith

My dad didn't have a penis
That is to say
I never saw it

It could well have lived happily
in the vast roominess
of his grey baggy work pants

I can't ever remember seeing my dad
go into or come out of a toilet
I'm not sure he ever took a bath

He tended to wash
his face and arms
in the kitchen sink

I exist – so he must have used
some form of penis
or penis substitute at least once

I presume his penis
if it existed
died

along with his other body parts
and was cremated and now lies
in ash particles

within the garden of rest
mingling with his other
post anatomical residue

unless individual atoms
have escaped and exist today
in say the petal of a magnolia blossom

or the cherry on the top of a Bakewell tart

I'm fairly sure my dad's penis
if actual
led a fairly invisible life all round

I know that no penis of his
ever slept in their bed
or any other bed
for seven years after
my mum died

I could hear my dad
sometimes at night
using his tear ducts
to release painkillers
to help him sleep

I have a photo of my dad
perhaps
with his young penis
in his smart suit trousers
at his wedding

I can't help but wonder
as I look at that picture
what life
his penis might have
imagined it would have

I'm told
by people who know these things
that my dad died of prostate cancer
which leads me to believe
his penis probably did exist

This amalgam of disparate elements
forming this nameable entity
seemed to do its duty
as far as function goes
for almost 90 years

I hope
along the way
some fun was had

Twelve raisins at the feast of St. Sylvester

Others may light up the night
with gunpowder

but I have been this way
before

Forgive me
if I lower my gaze a moment

I cannot think of twelves wishes
for the world

Even for those we love
twelve is only a start

It would take more than a day
to tell these to myself

The tears alone
could fill a year

Let us wish for one thing now
and consider that enough

one small thing
and both wish for it

each with all twelve wishes
to help make sure

You decide
the wish

I confess
I may be too scared

Friends, Romans, countrymen, lend me your ear defenders

The gentle vice
that keeps your head in place

Vault doors on the Safe Room
The clasp securing the jewels

Sonic drawbridges
guarding side gates

Binary black holes
holding a centre of gravity

Flood defence
against the rising waves

Matching comfort cushions
Personal Echo Chambers

Dual airlocks on a space station
Shields aligned

The world
on mute

We need a word

Maybe it depends what you want to achieve
with this word

You wouldn't say 'a person with blindness' would you?

Though does Autistic over emphasise Autism
beyond all other aspects of character

Maybe last week
when a mother
pulled her son from a public reading

instead

she could have turned to the old man who
complained that her child moved or jerked or danced too much
and said

He's Autistic
or
He has Autism
or
any word
that would have meant that she and her son
could have stayed in the room

and the old man
could have understood immediately

and later would have no need
to feel remorse

I have an eye infection
on the day of the magazine photo-shoot

To avoid the staples the photographer
wants to position the three of us off-centre

We are at home
but the sofa has been reset

The hearth is now hidden
the TV behind us

I'm positioned on a wooden chair
where I'd never sit

and asked to wear clothes
I wouldn't wear

to create a formal image
where we usually relax

I have become a refugee
in my own living room

Tilt your head this way
I'm told

Bend your arm the other
Hold still

Eyes
to camera

Now
act natural

As the flash explodes
like a gunshot to the head

Johnny lifts his hands to his ears
breaking the composition

his arms only inches higher
and he would be surrendering

Through genetic predisposition
I have gifted my son
his challenges

This doesn't seem so bleak
written black and white
on a page

Though over twenty years
carved into the day
with flesh and blood

the words tower
as we climb each morning
to reach the ground

Citing relationships that I know I will try to get close

It's hard to describe
as it has a language of its own

There's the love of a mother
for a son, of course

And the love of a son for a mother
Then there's more

A friendship like in a buddy movie
that you find hard to believe
could exist in real life

Elements of Morecambe and Wise
Jeeves and Wooster
even Thelma and Louise

Each part-coach, part-nurse, part-guardian-angel
part-hero, part-mentor, part-muse

Cajoling and bamboozling abound
Co-conspirators in cahoots

Foot soldiers
alone together under fire

A mother
and her autistic child

Yesterday was quite ordinary

We went through the usual wake up routine
Cornflakes, toast and peanut butter,
time on the computer, the iPad,
washed and dressed, word-search

The morning came and went without
much conscious thought
Johnny set the table for lunch
Filled three glasses with water

In the afternoon we went for a walk in the woods
Making something out of nothing
Angela used slowmo and timelapse
and we created little films for ourselves

Driving home we listened to music
Johnny set the table for dinner
Filled three glasses with water
and we all sat down together

I looked over to him, an 18 year old
with what might pass for designer stubble
Six foot four, muscular
a new haircut and suntan

and for no reason
I noticed
he was handsome
Hollywood handsome

We were eating dinner
quietly
like an ordinary family
I can't even remember what food

and there it was
a glimpse
unexpected
This was the man Johnny could have been

'Isn't Johnny handsome?' I said to Angela
wanting to include her in the moment
It was all I could do
to stop myself weeping like a fool

After
when I stacked the dishwasher alone
I broke like death

Unexpected
I hadn't glimpsed
the man Johnny could have been
The mourning was for a different loss

one known
but not understood until now
for there in this moment
was the beauty of the man he was

Pink stars in a blue sky

I don't have the imagination to paint
a swimming pool black

I was corralled into conformity
as a child

I love the boldness of the big red man
dominating a bright blue background

Orange on gold
and silver hills

I love
the bottom edges of paintings abandoned

I love
the untended drips

My son dances in the art gallery

I love
the innocence of a self-portrait in negative

with hair flying above the head
like personal rain

"How old was he when he first learnt to paint?"
An elderly lady asked

I reached for a book to share a photograph
of Johnny drawing when he was seven

"Just tell me" the woman barked
She had no interest in the photo

"Seven" I said "but more-so the last five years"
She retired to a seat in the corner

Her husband explained they had a grandson
who was autistic

"He doesn't paint at the moment"
the granddad added

Visitors to the exhibition filed past
already anticipating the next painting

The joyful colours
lit up the dull weather

The elderly lady sat alone for some time
and avoided eye contact

Her frame hung heavy
Her mind elsewhere

Tourist in my own landscape

How far down does the sun have to be
before you can call it a sunset?

We are some days past the solstice
enjoying early evening

and the star of the show
is reluctant to leave the stage

The balustrades on my patio
try to retain their grandeur

in the face of increasing insult
from all those with feathers

The zigzag of brickwork underfoot
is no longer illuminated

Ceramic pots overcrowded
await attention

The apple trees
are too full of fruit

Tomatoes and lettuces fall victim
to my inconsistency

The whole garden resembles
an old man in need of a haircut

I could write a well-kept garden
more easily
than perfect one

Final note on the fridge

Woke up dead
It was early so
I decided to let you lie in

Loaded the dishwasher
wiped the kitchen surfaces
emptied the bin

No point in shaving
until the morning of the funeral
– be fresher that way

Put the kettle on as if by instinct
took out two mugs before
I realised

Not sure how fast things go south
Opened a few windows
just in case

Keys are in my jacket
All the official papers
are in my office

Birth certificate you might need
Not to worry
there's no porn hidden away

My grey suit is hanging up
Maybe with the dark red tie
and that white shirt I never wore

Might just sit and look through
some old photos for a while
Hope that's alright

I can only view the universe from the inside
so nothing is certain

I have seen the shape of love
Felt it shift and drift like cloud

I've caught pain and let it go
leaving us both scarred

God I fear has got my measure
I don't think I will surprise him now

Thank you

Thank you to all those who've seen me before
and chosen to come again
Thank you to all those who took a chance
Thank you to all those who were dragged
along by a partner
or friend and have suffered stoically
(or not so stoically)

Thank you to all those who stayed to the end
Thank you to all those who sneaked off unnoticed
(or not so unnoticed)

Thank you to all those that laughed
Thank you to all those that didn't laugh but smiled
Thank you to all those that didn't laugh nor smile
but enjoyed themselves despite that

Thank you to all those that didn't laugh nor smile
and didn't enjoy themselves despite that

Thank you to all those intending to buy a book
Thank you to all those who've not decided yet
whether they intend to buy a book

Thank you to all those thinking
you can stick your books up your arse

Thank you to those who would like their book signed
Thank you to those who'd rather not have their book signed
as it's a gift and they haven't decided who it's for yet
and anyway it will probably end up on eBay

Thank you to those who think you can stick your signature
up your arse
with your book
and your pen

Thank you to those couples who buy a book together
and then feel uneasy that both their names are written on it
as they don't think their relationship is going to last

Thank you to those who hope the other partner
gets custody of the book

Thank you to those who think this entire poem
is just a way of reminding people about the books for sale

Thank you to those who will see me again sometime

Thank you to all those
who would rather eat their own earwax

Thank you to those who will follow me or like me
on Facebook

Thank you to those I've just reminded
to unfriend me or ban me from Facebook

Thank you to those who'd like a selfie
with me after the show
Thank you to those thinking
'who'd want a selfie with him?'

Thank you to those who wish
this last poem would have ended by now

Thank you to those who will applaud enthusiastically
at the end
quite possibly because it has ended

Thank you to those who will applaud
the appropriate amount so as not to stand out

Thank you to those who've become belligerent
over the course of this poem
and won't applaud at all

Thank you to the one person who will give me a standing ovation
then look around and think better of it

Thank you to my mum and dad, and your mums and dads
without whom this communication wouldn't exist

Thank you to any possible God, the universe
and the concepts of time and space

Thank you to those in a parallel universe
where this poem has already ended

Thank you to those in a parallel universe
where this poem never ends

Thank you to whoever or whatever put us in this particular universe
where this is the last line. Thank you